How Many Legs?

Learning to Multiply Using Repeated Addition

Kristine Lalley

Math
for the
REAL World™

Rosen Classroom Books & Materials
New York

Published in 2004 by The Rosen Publishing Group, Inc.
29 East 21st Street, New York, NY 10010

Book Design: Michael J. Flynn

Photo Credits: Cover © Nigel J. Dennis; Gallo Images/Corbis; p. 5 (mouse) © Clive Druett; Papilio/Corbis;
p. 5 (polar bear) © Tom Brakefield/Superstock; pp. 5 (chipmunk), 14 © David W. Hamilton/The Image Bank;
pp. 5 (elephant), 9 © Digital Stock; p. 7 © Steve Kaufman/Corbis; p. 11 © Wolfgang Kaehler/Corbis;
p. 13 © Danny Lehman/Corbis.

ISBN: 0-8239-8929-1
6-pack ISBN: 0-8239-7457-X

Manufactured in the United States of America

Contents

All Kinds of Animals

There are all kinds of animals that live on Earth. Some animals are big, like elephants and polar bears. Some animals are small, like chipmunks and mice. These animals might look very different, but they have one thing in common. They all have legs they use to move around!

These animals all have 4 legs, but not all animals have 4 legs. Some animals have 2 legs. Some animals have 6 legs. There are even some animals with 8 legs!

polar bear

mouse

chipmunk

elephant

5

The Ostrich

The **ostrich** is the largest bird on Earth. An ostrich can be up to 8 feet tall and weigh about 350 pounds! Even though it is a bird, an ostrich cannot fly because it is too heavy. However, an ostrich has 2 long legs that make it possible for the bird to run as fast as 40 miles per hour!

An ostrich has 2 legs. How many legs do 2 ostriches have?

We can add to find out.

$$\begin{array}{r} 2 \text{ legs} \\ + 2 \text{ legs} \\ \hline 4 \text{ legs} \end{array}$$

We can also **multiply** to get the answer.

$$\begin{array}{r} 2 \text{ legs} \\ \times 2 \\ \hline 4 \text{ legs} \end{array}$$

Adding 2 + 2 and multiplying 2 x 2 gives us the same answer: **4**

An ostrich has 2 feet. It has only 2 toes on each foot. How many toes does an ostrich have altogether? You can add or multiply to find out.

2 toes	2 toes
+ 2 toes	x 2
4 toes	4 toes

The Tallest Animal

Giraffes are the tallest animals on Earth. Some male giraffes can grow to be about 18 feet tall. Female giraffes are usually about 16 feet tall. One of the reasons giraffes are so tall is because they have very long legs. A giraffe's front legs are about 6 feet long. That's about as tall as a full-grown person!

A giraffe has 4 long legs. How many legs do 2 giraffes have?

We can add to find out.	We can also multiply to get the answer.
4 legs	4 legs
+ 4 legs	x 2
8 legs	8 legs

Adding 4 + 4 and multiplying 4 x 2 gives us the same answer: **8**

Giraffes live in Africa. They can go without drinking water for many weeks at a time.

The Grasshopper

Maybe you have seen a grasshopper in your backyard or in a park. Grasshoppers are **insects** and can be found in most parts of the world. Like other insects, grasshoppers have 6 legs. They can use their legs to jump about 20 times as far as the **length** of their body. That would be like a full-grown person jumping over 100 feet!

A grasshopper has 6 legs. How many legs do 2 grasshoppers have?

We can add to find out.	We can also multiply to get the answer.
6 legs	6 legs
+ 6 legs	x 2
12 legs	12 legs

Adding 6 + 6 and multiplying 6 x 2 gives us the same answer: **12**

A grasshopper has 5 eyes! How many eyes do 2 grasshoppers have? You can add or multiply to find out.

5 eyes + 5 eyes 10 eyes	5 eyes x 2 10 eyes

Spiders

Spiders are animals that have 8 legs. Most spiders make strong webs with **silk** they make inside their bodies. A spider uses its web to catch insects for food. A spider's web can be so strong that larger, stronger animals can't get free from the web once they have been caught in it.

A spider has 8 legs. How many legs do 2 spiders have?

We can add to find out.

$$8 \text{ legs}$$
$$+ \ 8 \text{ legs}$$
$$16 \text{ legs}$$

We can also multiply to get the answer.

$$8 \text{ legs}$$
$$\times \ 2$$
$$16 \text{ legs}$$

Adding 8 + 8 and multiplying 8 x 2 gives us the same answer: **16**

Female spiders are usually larger and
stronger than male spiders.

How Many Legs?

A zoo is a good place to see different kinds of animals. If you went to the zoo near the place where you live, maybe you would see some of the animals you have learned about in this book. Let's say you go to the zoo and see 3 ostriches. How many legs would the 3 ostriches have altogether? We can add or multiply to get the answer.

```
  2 legs
  2 legs
+ 2 legs
  6 legs
```

```
  2 legs
x 3
  6 legs
```

The 3 ostriches would have a **total** of 6 legs.

Glossary

insect (IN-sekt) Any one of a group of very small animals without bones and with bodies that are divided into 3 parts. Insects have 6 legs.

length (LENGTH) How long something is.

multiply (MUHL-tuh-ply) To add a number to itself a certain amount of times. For example, 4 times 2 means to add 4 two times.

ostrich (AHS-trich) The largest bird on Earth. Ostriches can run quickly but cannot fly.

silk (SILK) A soft, sometimes sticky thread that spiders spin from their bodies.

total (TOH-tuhl) The whole amount.

Index